TRUTH IS Stranger THAN FICTION

PEARSON
Prentice
Hall

Boston, Massachusetts
Upper Saddle River, New Jersey

ISBN 0-13-363636-4
1 2 3 4 5 6 7 8 9 10   11 10 09 08 07

Truth Is Stranger Than Fiction

Can truth always be proven?

Table of Contents

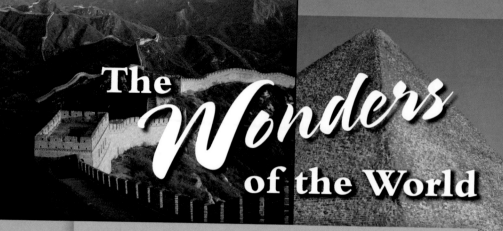

The *Wonders* of the World

For centuries, people have been making lists of the wonders of the world. There are lists about ancient wonders, natural wonders, modern engineering wonders, and more. Most of the wonders on the lists are "larger than life," such as a 100-foot-high statue!

Some of these wonders represent "truths" to the people who see them. For example, that very same statue was built to celebrate the survival of Rhodes after a siege by the Macedonians. The truth of the power of unity is represented by the larger-than-life statue that towered over the now-safe city. Can you guess the name of this wonder? Let's read to find out.

What Is a "Wonder"?

What makes something a **wonder**? The word itself means "a cause of awe or amazement." A wonder usually has great **significance**, or meaning, to the people who behold it. Those who see the wonder can **appreciate** its beauty. Or they can simply marvel at its size.

The Seven Wonders of the Ancient World

The most famous list of wonders is the Seven Wonders of the Ancient World. This list was originally created by ancient Greeks. However, it has varied over time. The wonders most often listed are seven larger-than-life structures. These creations were all made during a period from about 2575 B.C. to 280 B.C. The items on the list include only those that the ancient Greeks knew about and considered important. For example, the Great Wall of China is not on the Greeks' list of wonders.

| Wonders of the Ancient World ||
Wonders	Dates Built
Great Pyramid of Giza	c. 2589–2560 B.C.
Hanging Gardens of Babylon	c. 605–561 B.C.
Temple of Artemis	c. 550 B.C.
Statue of Zeus	c. 430 B.C.
Mausoleum of Halicarnassus	353–351 B.C.
Colossus of Rhodes	c. 282 B.C.
Pharos of Alexandria	280 B.C.

VOCABULARY

wonder (WUN duhr) *n.* something that makes you feel surprise and admiration

significance (sig NIF uh kuhnts) *n.* the meaning or importance of a thing, person, or idea

appreciate (uh PREE shee ayt) *v.* be grateful for; understand the meaning of something

5

Did These Wonders Exist?

Only one of the items on that list of ancient wonders still stands today. What proof is there that these other structures existed at all? Two ways that we can **establish** their existence are through written records and scientific discovery. Scholars learn about the seven ancient wonders from ancient texts. Archaeologists search for ruins and other physical **evidence** of the wonders.

The Great Pyramid of Giza The Great Pyramid of Giza in Egypt is the only ancient wonder still standing today. There are three giant pyramids at Giza. The oldest one was built for the Egyptian ruler Khufu, or Cheops as the Greeks called him. It is the only official ancient wonder. The other two are also magnificent, though, and many people include all three on the list. It took the efforts of around 100,000 people over a period of almost thirty years to build Khufu's pyramid.

Today, these great pyramids are all considered a **permanent** reminder of an amazing feat of engineering. They are a popular **destination** for many travelers.

The Hanging Gardens of Babylon The Hanging Gardens of Babylon is the only ancient wonder whose existence has not been proven. Writings from the 1st century B.C. tell of these gardens. One theory is that they were built by King Nebuchadnessar II, who reigned from about 605 to 561 B.C. **Legend** has it that he felt **compelled** to create the gardens for his wife, Amytis. **Evidently** she was homesick for the greenery of her former home. The descriptions say that these gardens grew on the roof of the royal palace of Babylon, an ancient city in what is now Iraq. Some archaeological evidence suggests that the gardens did really exist. No one will truly know until further evidence is found.

VOCABULARY

establish (uh STAB lish) v. determine; make sure of; set up

evidence (EV uh duhns) n. facts, objects, or signs that make you believe that something exists or is true

permanent (PER muh nuhnt) adj. lasting for all time

destination (des tuh NAY shuhn) n. place to which something is being sent or someone will arrive

legend (LEJ uhnd) n. a story handed down for generations among a people and believed to have historical basis

compelled (KUHM peld) v. forced; driven

evidently (ev uh DENT lee) adv. clearly; obviously; seemingly

The Great Pyramid of Giza consists of about 2 million blocks of stone. Each stone weighs more than two tons.

The Statue of Zeus at Olympia Created around 430 B.C. by the Greek sculptor Phidias, this statue was 40 feet high. Without today's technology, Phidias and his assistants had to **exert** great effort to build the tall statue. The statue is a tribute to the greatness of the Greek god Zeus. It shows him seated on a throne. Located in the Temple of Zeus at Olympia in Greece, the figure had skin of ivory and robes of gold. No one is certain of the fate of the statue. Most people believe that it was destroyed by fire. Images of the statue have been found on coins. This evidence tells us when the statue was built and what it looked like.

The Temple of Artemis at Ephesus This large temple honored Artemis. She was the Greek goddess of wild animals and hunting. First built around 550 B.C., the temple was known for its great size and beauty. Six years after it was built, it was destroyed by fire. The fire was set by a man named Herostratus. He wanted fame so desperately that he didn't care what it cost. The **challenge** of rebuilding the temple was met eventually, and a new temple was created. However, that temple was destroyed by invaders in A.D. 262 and not rebuilt again. Parts of the temple are now in the British Museum in London, England.

The Mausoleum of Halicarnassus Built around 350 B.C., the tomb of the ruler Mausolus was located in what is now Turkey. Its fame spread far and wide. In fact, the word *mausoleum,* which means "a building with a tomb," comes from this wonder. Evidently, an earthquake destroyed the tomb sometime between the 11th and 15th centuries. Today, parts of the tomb are found in London's British Museum.

The Colossus at Rhodes This huge statue of the sun god Helios stood in the ancient Greek city of Rhodes. The statue was built around 282 B.C. Descriptions say that it was more than 100 feet high. The people of Rhodes built it to celebrate the city's ability to withstand a siege by the **formidable** Macedonian army. The size of the statue surely was meant to **impress** people. It also was likely to remind

It was said that at night, ships could detect the light from the lighthouse at Alexandria up to 100 miles away.

those who saw it of the truth that unity and standing one's ground can win out over force. An earthquake destroyed the statue around 225 B.C. The ruins remained until the year A.D. 654. That year invaders broke up the statue. They sold its bronze supports for scrap.

VOCABULARY

exert (eg ZERT) *v.* put forth with force or energy

challenge (CHAL uhnj) *n.* a task requiring special effort; a dare to take part in a contest

formidable (FOHR muh duh buhl) *adj.* impressive; causing fear, dread, or awe

impress (im PRES) *v.* put pressure on; have a lasting effect in someone's memory

The Pharos of Alexandria This famous lighthouse, more than 350 feet high, was built about 280 B.C. It stood on Pharos, an island in the harbor of Alexandria, Egypt. At the time it was built, the pyramids at Giza were the only structures known to be taller. The lighthouse was destroyed as the result of earthquakes in the 1300s. Ruins of the lighthouse were discovered underwater by an archaeologist in 1994. These ruins prove that the lighthouse actually existed.

Other Ancient Wonders

There are many other wonders created long ago. The following larger-than-life creations appear on many lists of wonders. They still exist in one form or another today.

The Colosseum Completed in the year A.D. 82, this Roman arena seated 50,000 people. It was the site of horse races, games, and gladiator contests. Today its ruins still **reveal** how massive it was. Efforts are being made to restore the Colosseum. Plays and concerts have actually been staged there in the last decade.

The Catacombs of Alexandria An underground cemetery, these catacombs were built in the 2nd century A.D. They were built to honor the dead of Alexandria, Egypt. They consist of three levels built into solid rock. There is even an underground funeral banquet hall!

The Great Wall of China Construction of this 4,500 miles (7,300 km) of wall began in the 7th century B.C.

The Catacombs of Alexandria were discovered by accident. In 1900, a cart pulled by a donkey fell into a pit. The pit led to the underground cemetery.

It is actually a series of walls. They were built by individual Chinese states to keep out enemies. It is one of the biggest construction projects ever created.

Stonehenge Built in England around 3100 B.C., Stonehenge consists of a series of circles of gigantic stones. Many **mysteries** surround this wonder. For centuries, people have tried to understand how human beings with little technology were able to get those stones in

Vocabulary

reveal (ree VEEL) *v.* make known something hidden or kept secret

mystery (MIS tuh ree) *n.* something unexplained, unknown, or kept secret

The Porcelain Tower of Nanjing was one of the wonders of the world during the Middle Ages.

La Tour de PORCELLYNE   PORCELAIN TOOREN

In the 1990s, work was done to keep the Leaning Tower of Pisa from falling over. Soil was removed from under the raised end of the tower. It should stand for another 300 years.

place. Another mystery surrounds the actual purpose of this formation. It is believed to have been used for religious purposes, but no one knows for sure.

The Leaning Tower of Pisa Located in Pisa, Italy, this famous tilting marble bell tower dates to A.D. 1173. It was originally built to stand upright. However, it was built on soft ground. This has caused it to lean to one side over the years.

The Porcelain Tower of Nanjing This nine-story structure was built in the early 1400s in the ancient Chinese capital Nanjing. It was known as the Temple of Gratitude. Its white porcelain bricks and colorful tiles were destroyed over the years. Recent efforts to reconstruct it give hope that this excellent example of a Buddhist pagoda will be saved.

The Hagia Sophia at Constantinople This domed building was originally built in A.D. 532–537 as a Christian church in what is now Istanbul, Turkey. The name Sophia means "wisdom," and the church is often referred to as the Church of the Holy Wisdom. It became a mosque in the 15th century. At that time efforts were made to restore the building to its original splendor. It was eventually converted to a museum. Visitors come from all over the world to see this **magnificent** example of 6th-century architecture.

Vocabulary

magnificent (mag NIF uh sunt) *adj.* beautiful in a grand or stately way

The Channel Tunnel is one of the busiest railways in the world.

Wonders of the Modern World

Many of the ancient wonders were created to honor people or gods. In contrast, modern wonders are often created with usefulness in mind. With advances in engineering and technology, people can build structures that are taller and more amazing than ever before. These structures **evoke** feelings of awe in many who see them.

The American Society of Civil Engineers lists Seven Wonders of the Modern World. The list includes remarkable engineering successes of the 20th century. Unlike most of the ancient wonders, these structures can all be seen today.

The Channel Tunnel **Prior** to 1994, the only way to cross the English Channel was to take a boat, fly in a plane, or swim! The **quest** to find a quicker connection between Great Britain and the main continent of Europe was successful that year. A 31-mile-long tunnel under the English Channel opened. Passengers and their cars can now cross the English Channel in about 25 minutes on trains. These trains travel up to 100 miles per hour.

The CN Tower The CN Tower in Toronto, Canada, is currently the world's tallest free-standing structure. The antenna of the 1,815-foot tower transmits radio and television signals. It helps people **communicate** through modern technology. Opened to the public in 1976, the tower's observation deck has a glass floor. Standing on it, one has an amazing view of the ground!

The Empire State Building When it was completed in 1931, this New York City skyscraper was the tallest building in the world. Its design led to a **transformation** in cities around the world. Architects and builders would soon establish a new standard for creating skyscrapers. The 102-story building was completed in only one year and 45 days. The building is home to many businesses and is visited by tourists from around the world.

VOCABULARY

evoke (ee VOHK) *v.* draw a feeling, idea, or reaction out of someone

prior (PRY er) *adj.* coming before in time; earlier

quest (KWEST) *n.* a long search for something

communicate (kuh MYOO ni kayt) *v.* make ideas or feelings known

transformation (trans fohr MAY shun) *n.* a change in something or someone

The Empire State Building was the world's tallest building for more than forty years. It has been named by the American Society of Civil Engineers as one of the Seven Wonders of the Modern World.

The Golden Gate Bridge Upon its completion in 1937, California's Golden Gate Bridge was the world's tallest and longest suspension bridge. The beauty of the completed bridge would **exceed** the expectations of many people. The 1.2-mile-long bridge hangs from two main cables connected to two towers. The wire in the one-yard-thick cables could circle Earth three times!

The Itaipu Dam When building this dam, workers shifted the **previous** course of the Parana River, the world's seventh largest river. Completed in 1991, the dam is on the border of Brazil and Paraguay. It is one of the world's largest plants to **transform** water into power. It supplies 72% of Paraguay's energy. It also provides energy to parts of Brazil.

The Netherlands North Sea Protection Works The threat of flood is something people who live on land below sea level can **comprehend**. Without protection from the sea, much of the Netherlands would flood regularly during storm surges. The North Sea Protection Works consists of dams, barriers, and other measures to keep the Netherlands dry. In 1932 the first phase was completed.

VOCABULARY

exceed (ek SEED) v. go beyond the limit or standard
previous (PREEV ee uhs) adj. occurring before in time or order
transform (trans FOHRM) v. change
comprehend (kom pree HEND) v. grasp mentally; understand

The Golden Gate Bridge spans the entrance to San Francisco Bay. It connects the city of San Francisco with Marin County, California.

It consisted of a 19-mile-long dam that was 100 yards thick in places. Over the years, other parts of the network were added. The project was finally completed in 1986.

The Panama Canal For centuries, people had to travel around the tip of South America to sail from the Atlantic Ocean to the Pacific Ocean. The idea of creating a

Each year more than 14,000 ships pass through the Panama Canal, carrying more than 203 million tons of cargo.

shortcut sparked **intrigue** in many. In 1914, the Panama Canal opened, connecting the two oceans. This canal cut through a thin strip of land in the country of Panama. The engineers also created a dam to stop the Chagres River from flooding. Sadly, thousands of people died building the canal. Many died from malaria and other diseases. Nevertheless, the creation of the canal changed sea travel permanently.

V OCABULARY

intrigue (IN treeg) *n.* curiosity and interest

This picture shows an artist's idea of
what a future city might look like.

Wonders of the Future

What will people list as the future wonders of the
world? The size of an object may continue to impress
people in the future. Their lists might include biodome
cities, underwater cities, or space cities orbiting Earth.
Or people may select technological wonders for their
lists, such as the Internet, a force field, or cars that can
travel on land, air, and water.

Larger Than Life

People have **summoned** their most creative visions to meet the challenge of building these larger-than-life wonders of the past. Perhaps when something is large, it can reveal the truth in a way that an ordinary object cannot. In the future, though, we may find that the smallest things will seem the most wondrous, such as a microchip or a cell that holds the key to curing a disease. Large or small, the wonders of the world will always represent the universal experiences and hopes of people everywhere.

Discussion Questions

1. Why do you think that many of the wonders of the world are larger than life? Why do artists and builders create things that are so large? Why are people so impressed by size?

2. Do you think something large is more impressive than something small? Why or why not?

3. What things would you include on a list of Seven Wonders of the World? Make a list and compare it with a partner. Are the items on your list larger than life?

VOCABULARY

summoned (SUM uhnd) *v.* called together

Snakes are among the
most recognizable animals
in the world. We're used to
seeing them slither on the
ground, or even swim through
the water. If you think snakes
are creepy, how does it make
you feel to know that in the
jungles of Southeast Asia, there
are snakes that sail through the
air? Do these snakes really fly?
Let's find out!

SNAKES
in the SKY!

Flying Snakes: Fact or Fiction?

Think of the flying animals you know, and chances are that snakes don't come to mind. All sorts of birds and insects fly, of course. There's even a flying mammal—the bat. But flying snakes?

Winged snakes live in the make-believe world of myths and fairy tales. The best-known is the dragon, a flying snake that breathes fire. Everyone agrees that this is not the kind of thing you'll find in the real world. Snakes may slither on the ground or shimmy up a tree, but they don't sail through the air.

Or do they? As early as 1899, reports started coming from scientists visiting Southeast Asia about snakes that could "jump" from one tree to another.

On becoming airborne, the paradise tree snake flattens its body. This flattening doubles the snake's normal width.

People living in the area had long known about these snakes. In Malay, one of the local languages, they called the snake *ular terbang,* or "flying snake."

Scientists, however, did not have enough evidence to be sure that these snakes could actually fly. One thought the snake must be a kind of jumping cobra. As it turns out, he was **ignorant** of what these snakes could really do.

By 1931, observers in Malaysia were able to **verify** that these snakes could do more than just jump. In fact, in 1959, the owner of a tea plantation in India described seeing a snake fly out of a tree and sail over 50 yards through the air to its **destination** on the ground. If that's not a flying snake, then what is it?

This twin-barred tree snake glides through the air.

Do They Really Fly?

Once it was clear that "flying snakes" really exist, the question was: "How do they do it?" It turns out that flying snakes are like flying squirrels. They don't really fly. You'll never see either one of them leap from a tree, flap its wings, and soar up into the sky. Instead, they use their bodies to glide through the air.

Imagine an animal trapped out on a branch by a predator. Getting down safely is a real challenge. There are three basic choices: drop, fly, or glide. Dropping from a branch is easy, but it's not the best idea. As soon as it leaves the branch, the animal begins to **accelerate** through the air. With no way of controlling its fall, the animal keeps moving faster and faster. When it lands, it hits the ground hard.

Flying is a better solution. To be able to truly fly, an animal must be able to lift itself higher and higher into the air. Without wings, that's just not possible.

Gliding is a combination of dropping and flying. When the animal leaves the branch, it doesn't travel upward. It doesn't fall straight down, either. It travels out and away from the branch. Gliders can generate lift and slow themselves down in the air. That allows them to travel far and hit the ground without injuring themselves.

VOCABULARY

ignorant (IG nuh ruhnt) *adj.* not knowing facts or information

verify (VER uh fy) *v.* prove to be true

destination (des tuh NAY shuhn) *n.* place to which something is being sent or someone will arrive

accelerate (ak SEL uhr ayt) *v.* speed up

One characteristic of a glider is that it travels farther horizontally than it does vertically. Let's say an animal leaps from a tree branch that's twenty feet high. If it's a glider, it will usually travel more than twenty feet away from the tree before it lands.

Snakes and Other Gliders

Most gliding animals have something on their bodies that catches the air like a sail or parachute. This helps them glide through the air instead of dropping straight to the ground. Flying squirrels have flaps of skin that connect their front and back legs. When they leap from a tree, they spread their legs wide, stretching out the skin. Flying frogs have extra-large webbed feet that help them stay aloft. Another glider, the flying lizard *Draco*, has skin flaps that it can open up like an umbrella. This allows it to travel more than a hundred feet through the air! Skilled gliders also use their "wings" to **adjust** their path in flight.

Snakes, however, have no arms, no legs, and no skin flaps to spread. In order to glide, a snake has to find a way to **transform** its long skinny body into a flying machine. Since the snake has no wings to work with, it **distorts** its body instead.

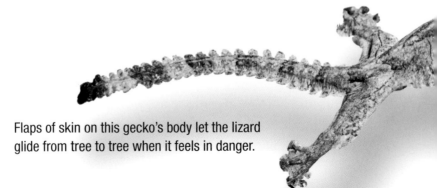

Flaps of skin on this gecko's body let the lizard glide from tree to tree when it feels in danger.

This Southern flying squirrel can glide up to 150 feet (46 m) and steers with its tail. It lands by gripping a tree trunk with all four feet.

Once it is airborne, the snake opens its ribcage and flattens itself. With its weight spread out over a larger surface, it slows its fall and begins to glide. As it glides, it slithers through the sky. From the side, it looks like a flying ribbon. When the snake lands, it pulls its **resilient** body back into its normal shape and slithers away.

Vocabulary

adjust (uh JUHST) *v.* change in order to fit or feel comfortable

transform (trans FOHRM) *v.* change

distort (di STORT) *v.* twist an object or idea out of shape

resilient (ree ZIL yuhnt) *adj.* able to spring back into shape

More to Know and Learn

Scientists have learned many basic facts about flying snakes since they were first observed. One thing is now clear: the "flying snake" is actually five different kinds of snakes. They all belong to the same genus, or grouping of snakes, called *Chrysopelea*. The two flying snakes that we know the most about are the golden tree snake and the paradise tree snake.

▲ The paradise tree snake glides well. It can guide its body through the air.

◄ The golden tree snake does not glide well, but it doesn't just fall straight down.

Flying snakes are generally pretty small. Most adults are no more than four feet long. The twin-banded tree snake doesn't grow to be much more than two feet. This snake, like the other *Chrysopelea* snakes, can climb trees by using its belly scales to grip onto tree bark. If the bark is not rough enough, however, the snake will slip down when it tries to climb.

Scientists aren't sure whether the *Chrysopelea* snakes sleep in the treetops. They do know that they eat the small animals they find up there: usually lizards, but also small birds, bats, and perhaps frogs. No one knows for sure which animals prey on these snakes. Some scientists think that the snakes' gliding helps them **survive** by avoiding predators.

The "flying snakes" have small fangs in the back of their mouths. Although the fangs are only a couple of millimeters long, they are **adequate** for injecting the snakes' prey with venom. Although the venom is deadly to the prey, it's not harmful to humans.

All flying snakes are native to Asian rain forests. Some are kept in captivity, although they don't make very good pets. The golden tree snake, in particular, doesn't **react** well to being handled and is a real biter. No matter where the snakes are, they **require** room to climb, jump, and glide.

VOCABULARY

survive (ser VYV) *v.* outlive or live beyond a life-threatening event or illness

adequate (AD i kwuht) *adj.* enough for what is required or needed

react (re AKT) *v.* behave in a particular way in response to someone or something

require (ree KWYR) *v.* demand by law; deem as necessary

How Can a Snake Stay in the Air?

Before entering the University of Chicago as a biology graduate student, Jake Socha heard Robert Dudley of the University of Texas mention flying snakes. He noted that little was known about them. Socha was **intrigued** by the idea of flying snakes. How did they stay in the air? Socha began searching for the answer. His goal was to **comprehend** how these snakes were able to glide.

By the time Socha began his studies in the 1990s, there was no longer any doubt that flying snakes existed. But beyond that, there were a lot of questions to be answered. Most importantly, how is the snake able to stay in the air? To find out, Socha began performing experiments with the snakes.

Socha was not the first person to experiment with flying snakes. Scientists had discovered that the snakes needed to be taken to a high place. Once there, they could launch themselves and sail down to the ground.

Experiments show that the higher the launch pad, the longer the flight. Another pair of scientists took the snakes to the top of a 130-foot-tall tower. From there, the snakes could glide as far as 100 feet. The scientists also dropped non-flying snakes to see whether they would glide, too. (They didn't.)

Studying the Snakes in Flight

In his experiments, Socha used only flying snakes. He took them to the highest places he could find that had safe landing spots. At first, he used buildings that had lawns nearby. Socha built small boxes that the snakes

This is a multiple-exposure of a paradise tree snake. It shows how the snake forms a loop with its body as it launches itself into the air.

could use as launch pads. He never needed to throw the snakes; they always launched themselves.

The buildings were adequate at first. But as he learned more about the snakes, Socha changed his launch setup. He built tall metal towers with platforms at the top. Then, he placed a branch on the platform that the snake could use to launch itself. Since this was more like a tree, it would give a better picture of how the snake would act in the wild.

VOCABULARY

intrigue (in TREEG) *v.* arouse curiosity and interest

comprehend (kom pree HEND) *v.* grasp mentally; understand

31

Photographer Tim Laman records a snake's jumping takeoff behavior.

There was another good thing about the towers. They allowed Socha to place cameras that could film the snakes from launch pad to touch down. Socha hoped the cameras would **reveal** the secrets of the snakes' flight.

To better understand their flight, he also painted stripes on the head, middle, and end of each snake's body. This made it easier to tell what happened to the snake as it flew. Socha worked with a partner to combine all this information into a three-dimensional model of the snake in flight.

With Katie LaBarbera's
help, Jake Socha marks the
back part of a snake with paint.

VOCABULARY

reveal (ree VEEL) *v.* make known something hidden or
kept secret

33

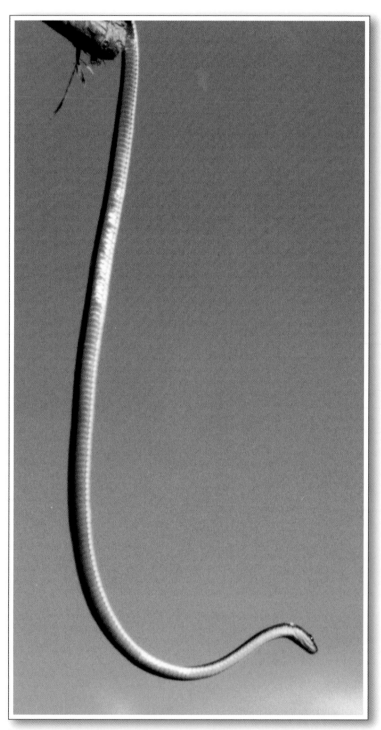

This twin-barred tree snake forms a J-loop
during takeoff from a branch.

It Starts with J and Ends with S

Usually, Socha could get a snake to jump just by getting too close to it. If that didn't work, he'd prod it gently to try to get it to move. If the snake still didn't **respond** after a few minutes, it was taken off the branch.

When a snake was ready to go, it hung from the branch like a living letter J. Then, it would fling itself up into the air and begin to fall. This first stage of the snake's flight is known as the "ballistic dive."

After falling for about ten feet, the snake would change into an S-shape and begin to slither in mid-air. The snake would also flatten its body, so that it took the shape of a sideways C. Doing this helped slow the snake down. It also decreased the snake's glide angle.

You can think of a glide angle like this. If you're dropping straight down, your glide angle is ninety degrees. On the other hand, if you're flying in a straight line and not moving down at all, your glide angle is zero. The lower your glide angle, the farther you can glide. Socha found that the snakes could get their glide angle as low as thirteen degrees. He was **impressed**—they were much better gliders than people had suspected! The longest flight that Socha recorded **exceeded** sixty feet. Each glide lasted about two seconds.

Vocabulary

respond (ree SPAHND) *v.* reply or act in answering

impress (im PRES) *v.* put pressure on; have a lasting effect in someone's memory

exceed (ek SEED) *v.* go beyond the limit or standard

More Flying Snake Facts

Socha's research helped **clarify** other details about snakes in flight. The cameras showed that after their initial dive, the snakes kept their heads down as they traveled. Socha also discovered that snakes that form bigger bends when they slither move through the air faster.

Socha found out two other important things about flying snakes. For one, the paradise tree snake is a much better glider than the golden tree snake. On average, the paradise tree snake can travel twice as far. It also falls more slowly and has a lower glide angle.

The other thing Socha discovered is that smaller snakes can glide farther than bigger ones. Socha found one exception to this, though, when he used a snake that was still very young. He found that it couldn't glide as far as some of the adult snakes. It glided well enough, though, that Socha concluded that the snakes probably know how to glide as soon as they hatch.

What's Still Mysterious about These Snakes?

So, flying snakes really do exist. And thanks to Jake Socha's work, we know much more about their **uncanny** glid-ing abilities than we used to. However, there are still lots of questions to answer.

For one thing, how did these snakes evolve the ability to fly? One possibility is that it's easier to go from tree to tree in the air. The snakes have to **exert** less energy than they would if they slithered down one tree, crawled along the ground, and then climbed up another one. It also may be safer for the snakes. After all, gliding is a pretty good way to escape a predator.

We know more about what these snakes eat. But can they catch prey in mid-air? No one has seen a flying snake do this, but they glide well enough that it's certainly possible.

We now know how the snakes flatten their bodies when they glide. But when they do it, what happens to their organs? And if a snake has just finished eating, can it still glide as well?

VOCABULARY

clarify (KLAR uh fy) *v.* make clear
uncanny (uhn KAN ee) *adj.* strange; eerie
exert (eg ZERT) *v.* put forth with force or energy

This golden tree snake is preparing to take off from a branch.

We've seen that snakes slither as they move through the air. But why do they do it? Does it help them keep their balance as they glide? Or do they just do it because that's how they're used to traveling on land? No doubt, *someone* will be intrigued enough to try to find the answers to these questions. Perhaps, that someone will be you!

Twin-barred tree snakes like this one don't glide as well as paradise tree snakes.

Discussion Questions

1. Do you think creatures such as fire-breathing dragons are the invention of the human imagination, or are they based on real animals, such as flying snakes? Explain your thoughts on this.

2. Why do you think scientists doubted that the snakes could really fly? Were they right to have doubts?

3. Has Jake Socha's research made the snakes more mysterious or less mysterious? Give reasons to explain your answer.

REEL TIME HOW THE MOVIES PORTRAY HISTORY

Some of the most successful Hollywood movies ever made have been historical films. These larger-than-life epics on the big screen have attracted fans since movies first began. There's something about being transported to another time and place that audiences find magical. What most people watching a historical film don't see are the blood, sweat, and tears behind the magic. Making history come alive on-screen requires a lot of preparation and dedication. Luckily, there are plenty of people in Hollywood willing to do just that.

The audience has a role to play as well. Good historical films **require** a suspension of disbelief. Viewers watching a movie that takes place in ancient Greece know that it wasn't really filmed in ancient times. Yet, if the movie is made well, viewers allow the movie to **deceive** them. They believe they are seeing ancient Greece on screen.

How do moviemakers perform this amazing feat? It's a **challenge** that involves hard work—and often a cast and crew of thousands—to pull off. Attention must be paid to every detail: how characters looked, talked, and felt; how places looked; how events really happened; what the weather was like.

The result is worth it, though. For two hours (more or less) viewers are transported to a different time and place. That's as close to a time machine as any of us is likely to come.

VOCABULARY

require (ree KWYR) *v.* demand by law; deem as necessary

deceive (dee SEEV) *v.* make someone believe something that is not true

challenge (CHAL uhnj) *n.* a task requiring special effort; a dare to take part in a contest

In *Elizabeth,* Cate Blanchett played Queen Elizabeth I of England (top). In *Glory,* Robert Gould Shaw, played by Matthew Broderick, leads the Civil War's first all-black volunteer company (left).

A Moviemaking Primer

How **fluent** are you in the language of moviemaking? Take a look at some of the terms below.

director: the person in artistic control of the movie. The director controls the actors, the set, and the filming.

producer: the boss of the movie. A producer often does most of the hiring on a set. A producer also raises money.

extras: people who appear in movies but are not specific characters and speak no lines. Extras are usually parts of crowds or in the background of scenes. Most epic films use a lot of extras.

scene: a piece of a screenplay or story that is set in a particular location. Movie shoots are usually broken down into scenes.

Recreating History

A lot of work goes into trying to **recreate** history on-screen. It would be almost impossible to describe every part of making a historical film. However, some things are more important than others. Let's look at a few of the more important parts of historical filmmaking.

The picture shows the film set in a scene from *The Last Emperor*. The movie was shot on location in China.

VOCABULARY

fluent (FLOO uhnt) *adj.* able to write or speak easily and smoothly

recreate (ree kree AYT) *v.* make something from the past exist again in a new form or be experienced again

The Set

In a historical film, all the scenes not shot on location are shot on a set. This means that the production designers (or set designers) play a key role in the movie. Their job is to **establish** the look and feel of a particular time.

Most set designers do a lot of research before coming up with sketches of what a set might look like. They work closely with the director to ensure that everyone's vision of how the film should look is the same.

This picture shows the set of a French village in *Saving Private Ryan*.

One **benefit** of shooting on a set compared to shooting on location is that the moviemakers have more control. They can make things just as they want them and **adjust** them if they need to. This is what happened with *Troy*. Production designer Nigel Phelps worked with director Wolfgang Petersen to create the city of Troy just as both men envisioned it.

Sets can also be more economical than locations. In the World War II movie *Saving Private Ryan,* an entire French village was recreated on a set in England. The same set was then used in a new **context** in the movie to represent a different French village.

Vocabulary

establish (uh STAB lish) *v.* determine; make sure of; set up

benefit (BEN uh fit) *n.* a gain; positive result

adjust (uh JUHST) *v.* change in order to fit or feel comfortable

context (KON tekst) *n.* the background or environment of a particular event or location

The Costumes and Props

Many people refer to historical films as costume dramas, and with good reason. Costumes and props help **reveal** a movie's historical period. They can **communicate** a time period to audiences almost better than anything else. Are there hoop skirts on-screen? Then the movie must be set in the mid–1800s. Are the men wearing togas? Think of ancient Rome.

Costume designers often go to great lengths to make sure their costumes are accurate or just the way they

want them. The costumers on *Elizabeth* worked off the queen's coronation portrait to be sure they got her dress right. Director Sofia Coppola had hundreds of pair of shoes made for her film *Marie Antoinette.*

Computer Generated Imagery (CGI)

CGI refers to special effects done on the computer. Today, most historical films use CGI to help create their sense of scale or history. CGI can be used to eliminate unwanted modern details from a historical backdrop. It can be used to make seemingly impossible things happen.

CGI can also be used to add extras to a scene. In the battle scene that opens *Gladiator,* CGI was used to add soldiers to the scene.

VOCABULARY

reveal (ree VEEL) *v.* make known something hidden or kept secret

communicate (kuh MYOO ni kayt) *v.* make ideas or feelings known

Actress Kirsten Dunst wears clothing like Marie Antionette, Queen of France, would have worn in the late 1700s.

Epic Films

Perhaps the most popular historical movies are **epic** films. Epics recreate events on a large scale. They tend to tell stories that cover a period of many years. Though most epics are based on history, epic films are not always accurate. They often **distort** historical events and omit important facts in the name of drama.

Epic films are usually very expensive to make. Their large, sweeping stories require huge casts and elaborate costumes. A lot of money is spent trying to **evoke** a particular time period. Epics are often shot both on location and on huge sets built just for the movie.

Epic films have been around since moviemaking first began. There are many **fantastic** silent movie epics. One of the first, considered by some to be one of the greatest silent movies, was D. W. Griffith's *Intolerance,* released in 1916. This movie tells four different stories that span hundreds of years.

Another great silent epic is the version of *Ben-Hur* released in 1925. The film took two years, millions of dollars, and a cast of thousands to make. It was the most expensive silent film ever made.

Since then, of course, epic movies have gotten more elaborate and more expensive. However, that has not stopped film studios from feeling **compelled** to make them. Take a look at a few epic movies that continue to **impress** audiences.

Ramon Navarro plays Ben-Hur in the 1925 silent film.

VOCABULARY

epic (EP ik) *adj.* telling a story that is long and full of action; based on an epic poem, which tells the story of what gods or important people did in ancient times

distort (di STORT) *v.* twist an object or idea out of shape

evoke (ee VOHK) *v.* draw a feeling, idea, or reaction out of someone

fantastic (fan TAS tik) *adj.* extremely good; imaginative; incredible

compelled (KUHM peld) *v.* forced; driven

impress (im PRES) *v.* put pressure on; have a lasting effect in someone's memory

49

Gone With the Wind (1939) Clocking in at almost four hours, this American classic is one of the longest movies ever released. The movie is set in the South before, during, and after the Civil War. To tell its epic story required 50 speaking roles and 2,400 extras. From the acting to the costumes to the sets, this film **awed** audiences and won ten Academy Awards.

The first scene to be shot for the movie—and one of the most famous—was the burning of Atlanta. No fire scene on this scale had ever been attempted before. Old sets from the studio were set ablaze on a 40-acre studio backlot. The fire shot 500 feet high in the air. It took 15,000 gallons of water to quench the flames after filming stopped. Stand-ins played the roles of the lead characters during this scene's filming.

Ben-Hur (1959) Considered by some people to be the best epic ever, this three-and-a-half-hour remake of the 1925 version was the most expensive film ever made at the time. It took more than six years of planning and six months of filming to tell the story of **intrigue** and rivalry between two old friends in Jerusalem. The efforts were worth it, though. *Ben-Hur* won eleven Academy Awards.

The most famous scene in the film, and the one that audiences **appreciate** the most, is the chariot race sequence. For the chariot race, a complete replica of the Circus Maximus in Rome was created on a studio backlot. Eighteen chariots were created, and 15,000 extras were hired to play spectators. The race took five weeks to film.

Despite all the work, none of the movie's spectacular sets remain. The studio was afraid that another movie-maker might use one of the sets as a **background** for another film. So all the sets were destroyed after the movie was completed.

In the 1959 version of *Ben-Hur*, Charlton Heston competes in the chariot race.

VOCABULARY

awed (AWD) *v.* inspired a feeling of fear and wonder

intrigue (IN treeg) *n.* curiosity and interest

appreciate (uh PREE shee ayt) *v.* be grateful for; understand the meaning of something

background (BAK grownd) *n.* part of a movie scene that is or appears to be toward the back

Titanic (1997) This almost three-hour movie was based on the real-life sinking of the ship *Titanic* in 1912. The movie took two years to film and cost $250 million. It won eleven Academy Awards.

To make the story seem **realistic**, director James Cameron decided to film the remains of the actual *Titanic,* which lay on the bottom of the ocean floor. He had his brother design a special deep-sea camera for the job. However, the camera held only 12 minutes of film. It took 12 dives to get all the footage Cameron needed.

Most of *Titanic* was shot on a set in Mexico. A replica of the ship was built in a specially designed tank on the set. To make the set authentic, the companies who had decorated the original ship were hired to do the set decor.

Huge amounts of water were used during filming. In one scene while the ship is sinking, more than 120,000 tons of water crash through a wall!

Unlike *Gone With the Wind* or *Ben-Hur,* this blockbuster relied on CGI to **transform** scenes and make history come alive. Many of the people and backgrounds in *Titanic* are computer-generated imagery.

VOCABULARY

realistic (ree uh LIS tik) *adj.* showing things as they are or were in real life

transform (trans FOHRM) *v.* change

This scene from *Titanic* was filmed on the wreck of the real sunken ship.

Troy (2004)

This film uses great sets and CGI to take audiences back thousands of years to the Trojan War, an epic battle between the ancient Greeks and the Trojans. A lot of research went into figuring out how to make the city of Troy come alive. The set, built in Mexico, included a 40-foot by 500-foot wall, made from 200 tons of plaster.

The actors, too, had a part to play in making history seem real. Actor Brad Pitt worked for months to learn sword fighting and to put on the muscle that would give him an **uncanny** resemblance to a Greek statue.

Perhaps the most amazing scenes in the movie were filmed on a four-mile-long Mexican beach. It was the perfect location, except for one problem. The beach

This scene from *Troy* shows the Trojan Horse being taken into the city of Troy.

housed 4,000 special, protected cacti. Botanists had to be called in to transplant the cacti to a nursery. When filming was finished, all the plants had to be replaced in the same spots from which they had been dug.

Oops! What's That Doing There?

In a historical film, not everything is perfect. Production crews try to make the movie as realistic as possible. Occasionally, however, they mess up. Things pop up that don't belong in the film's historical period. These are known as anachronisms. Here are a few anachronisms from some famous historical films.

- In *Gone With the Wind,* a lamppost with a lightbulb is shown. Lightbulbs didn't exist during the period in which the movie takes place.
- In *Ben-Hur,* during the chariot race, one of the trumpeters is wearing a watch. Watches didn't exist in biblical times.
- In *Titanic,* a present-day world map is shown in the radio room of the ship. A 1912 world map would have looked very different, since many countries' borders changed during the 20th century.
- In *Troy,* a wounded Paris gets stitches. The problem with this is that sewing up wounds didn't become common until thousands of years after the Trojan War.
- In *Gladiator,* one of the spectators in the Colosseum is wearing modern sunglasses!

VOCABULARY

uncanny (uhn KAN ee) *adj.* strange; eerie

The Future of Historical Films

Today's audiences are as enchanted by historical films as any audiences of the past. Films like *Titanic* and *Gladiator* were enormous box-office successes, and everyone knows that Hollywood likes to **emulate** its own success. That means that epic blockbusters are sure to be a **permanent** part of the movie world. What audiences don't know is which historical period the next epic movie will **focus** on.

Hollywood isn't telling—yet.

Discussion Questions

1. Historical films often cost a lot to make. Discuss what goes into making a historical film. Why do you think they are so expensive?

2. Why do audiences like historical films so much? What do they give audiences that other movies can't? What do historical films do that historical books can't do?

3. Technology has changed the way historical films are made. How has it changed the way audiences think of and view these films?

VOCABULARY

emulate (EM yoo layt) *v.* equal by imitating or copying

permanent (PER muh nuhnt) *adj.* lasting for all time

focus (FOH kuhs) *v.* fix or concentrate on one thing; adjust to make clear

Peter O'Toole plays the tutor to the Chinese Emperor Pu Yi in *The Last Emperor.*

MATH TRICKS

by David Heath

"Pick a card. Any card!" With great showmanship, the magician **resumes** shuffling and reshuffling the deck of cards. At last, a card is taken from the top of the deck. It is, of course, the card chosen by the audience member. It seems remarkable, but we all know that it isn't magic, just a trick. For centuries, magicians have been performing sleight of hand tricks to entertain audiences. The success of many of the best tricks involves mathematics—sometimes simple counting, other times probability, or algebra. As **incredible** as some of these tricks appear, they are based on simple mathematical principles and **strategies**. Would you like to learn some math tricks and **impress** your friends?

Math Tricks with Basic Operations

There are many tricks that you can perform using math. Some tricks are based on the four basic arithmetic operations: addition, subtraction, multiplication, and division. Other tricks are created using more complicated algebraic functions. All of them, however, are fun and easy to learn if you **invest** a little time and effort. WARNING: YOU CAN DO ALL OF THESE TRICKS WITHOUT ADULT SUPERVISION!

I've Got Your Number This trick can amaze even the most **mature** members of your audience—the ones who think they've seen it all. They'll think you can predict what they're going to write. Before you launch into this trick, double the current year and write that sum on a slip of paper. Fold it up, and put it into your pocket. Give your friend a pencil and piece of paper and then follow the instructions.

VOCABULARY

resumed (ree ZOOMD) *v.* began again; continued

incredible (in KRED uh buhl) *adj.* unbelievable; amazing

strategy (STRAT uh jee) *n.* set of plans used to gain succes or achieve an aim

impress (im PRES) *v.* put pressure on; have a lasting effect in someone's memory

invest (in VEST) *v.* put time, effort, or money into something for a profit or return

mature (muh CHER/TOHR) *adj.* behaving in a reasonable way; considered like an adult

Instructions for I've Got Your Number

Step 1: Write down the year you were born.

Step 2: Write down the year you started school.

Step 3: Write down how old you will be at the end of the current year.

Step 4: Write down the number of years you have been in school at the end of this current school year.

Step 5: Add the four numbers.

When the addition is complete, show your friend the number you wrote on the piece of paper in your pocket. It will be the same number! It seems **uncanny**, but it's really not. Let's analyze how this works. If you add the year you were born with your age at the end of the current year, the sum will be the current year. The same thing is true when you add the year you started school with the number of years you've been in school. Adding those numbers together is the same as adding the current year to itself.

This trick also works for older people who have already graduated from high school. You just have to change the questions to identify the important information. Ask them to write down the year they were born, the year they graduated from high school, their age at the end of this year, and the number of years since graduation at the end of this year.

Fooling Around Here's a fun trick that uses some very simple calculations to achieve interesting results. The numbers are large, so it would be a **challenge** to do this trick without a calculator.

Instructions for Fooling Around

Step 1: Pick a three-digit number where the first and third digits differ by at least two and no two digits are the same.

Step 2: Reverse the digits and subtract the smaller number from the larger number.

Step 3: Reverse the digits to the answer to Step 2, and add the two numbers together.

Step 4: Multiply the sum by 1,000,000.

Step 5: Subtract 733,361,573 from the answer to Step 4.

Step 6: Reverse the digits to the answer to Step 5.

Step 7: Write letters under the digits, using this code to **interpret** the message—0=Y, 1=M, 2=P, 3=L, 4=R, 5=O, 6=F, 7=A, 8=I, 9=B.

Try this trick a couple times and check the results of each step. You'll soon realize that you always obtain a result with a digit sum of 9 in Step 2, so the number you start with makes no difference as long as the first and third digits differ by more than two and no two digits are the same. You can start **improvising** with different numbers and come up with your own trick.

VOCABULARY

uncanny (uhn KAN ee) *adj.* strange; eerie

challenge (CHAL uhnj) *n.* a task requiring special effort; a dare to take part in a contest

interpret (in TER pruht) *v.* explain the meaning of something; translate

improvising (IM pruh VYZ ing) *v.* making up or inventing on the spur of the moment

A Kangaroo in Denmark Here's another trick where you predict what a friend is thinking. This one is based a little on probability, where you have to assume your friend will come up with the most **obvious** answers for your directions.

Instructions for A Kangaroo in Denmark
  Step 1: Think of a number from 2 to 10.
  Step 2: Multiply that number by 9.
  Step 3: Add the digits together.
  Step 4: Subtract 5 from the sum of the digits from Step 3.
  Step 5: Identify the letter that matches the number (1=A, 2=B, 3=C, etc.).
  Step 6: Think of a country that starts with that letter.
  Step 7: Think of an animal that starts with the last letter of your country.
  Step 8: Think of a color that starts with the last letter of your animal.

When your friend has come up with all the related information ask, "Are you thinking about an orange kangaroo in Denmark?" More than likely, you'll be right.

Let's evaluate how it works: When you multiply any number from 2 to 10 by 9, the sum of the digits of the product will always equal 9. You may **recall** your math teacher telling you this in the fourth grade. So when you subtract 5 from the sum of the digits (9), you'll end up with a difference of 4. Four equals the letter *D*, therefore, the country will always begin with *D*. There are five countries that begin with *D*—Denmark, Dhekelia, Djibouti, Dominica, and the Dominican Republic.

Map of Denmark

This will **restrict** your friend's choices. Chances are, your friend will choose Denmark. Kangaroos are the most common animals beginning with *K,* and orange is the most common color beginning with *O.* If you can figure out a way to make your friends cooperate with you and choose the most obvious answers, you'll always predict their answers correctly. You can try a variation of this trick by changing Step 7 to "Think of an animal that starts with the second letter of your country." The second letter is *E,* so chances are good that your friend will choose an elephant.

VOCABULARY

obvious (AHB vee uhs) *adj.* easy to see or understand; plain; evident

recall (re CAWL) *v.* call back to mind; remember

restrict (ree STRIKT) *v.* keep within limits

Albert Einstein on his
72nd birthday

You're a Real Einstein People **acquainted** with Albert Einstein say he loved to make up math tricks. Here is one of the tricks he liked to play on his friends. See how well you can **emulate** this math genius.

Before you begin, write the number 1,089 on a slip of paper, fold it up, and hand it to your friend. Don't let your friend see what you've written on the paper. Then have the friend follow the instructions.

Instructions for You're a Real Einstein
  Step 1: Choose a three-digit number, in which the first and last digits differ by at least two.
  Step 2: Reverse the digits.
  Step 3: Subtract the lesser number from the greater.
  Step 4: Reverse the digits in the number from Step 3.
  Step 5: Add the reversed number to the number from Step 3.

Then have your friend look at the number you wrote on the paper. It will be the same number that resulted from your friend's calculations—1,089. When you follow the steps correctly, the answer to Step 3 will always produce a 3-digit number with a digit sum of 9. When you reverse those digits and add the two numbers, the answer can only be 1,089.

Talking Calculators

Calculators are amazing tools. They are like miniature computers in your hands. You probably use a calculator to add, subtract, multiply, divide, find square roots, and such. The **benefit** of using a calculator is incalculable. But did you know that if you **focus** on certain numbers upside-down they **transform** into letters? Look at this table. It shows calculator numbers and the letters they form when you turn your calculator around.

0	O	3	E	6	g
1	I	4	h	7	l
2	Z	5	S	8	B

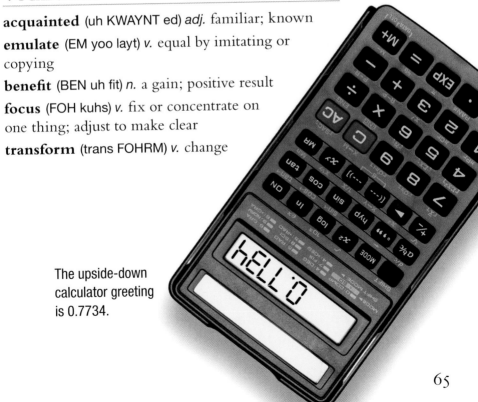

The upside-down calculator greeting is 0.7734.

Using these letters, you can create words with your calculator. Below are just a few of the numbers that translate into words when you look at them upside-down on a standard calculator.

34 = he	663 = egg	604 = hog
335 = see	7738 = bell	5507 = loss
77345 = shell	376616 = giggle	5318804 = hobbies

You can make up riddles or puzzles using calculator words. Here's an example:

There was a very wealthy person who loved cars. In fact, this person owned 71 cars (key in 71 on the calculator). But, one by one, they stopped running until there were only 5 left (multiply 71 by 5). He took them to two different mechanics, and they both said that all the cars were missing a **vital** element (multiply 355 by 2). Then turn the calculator upside down to reveal the answer: "The rich man had **ignored** the fact that his cars needed oil."

Try your hand at making up a riddle. First start with a number that can be read upside-down as a word. Next, break the number into factors or simply separate it into num-bers that can be added together to equal the word/number. Finally, make up some sort of story or riddle to go with the numbers.

66

Algebra Is the Answer

There are many tricks that appear to just use the basic operations. The reason they work, however, is that they **require** algebra. It is fun to do the tricks even if you are **ignorant** of why they work. But to understand the algebraic formulas behind the tricks is a trick in itself.

This last series of tricks can all be explained using algebra.

Make That Five Here's another trick where you can predict the answer to a series of calculations, no matter what numbers your friends contribute. Here's what you have your friends do.

Instructions for Make That Five

Step 1: Pick any number.

Step 2: Add the next greater number to the original number.

Step 3: Add 9 to the sum of the other two numbers.

Step 4: Divide the sum of Step 3 by 2.

Step 5: Subtract the original number.

VOCABULARY

vital (VYT uhl) *adj.* extremely important; necessary

reveal (ree VEEL) *v.* make known something hidden or kept secret

ignored (ig NOHRD) *v.* paid no attention to

require (ree KWYR) *v.* demand by law; deem as necessary

ignorant (IG nuh ruhnt) *adj.* not knowing facts or information

The answer will always be 5. You can demonstrate how you came to this answer by looking at it algebraically.

Let x = the number picked by the friend

$x + (x + 1) = 2x + 1$

$2x + 10$

$x + 5$

5

Birthday Algebra Although this trick just uses the four basic operations—addition, subtraction, multiplication, and division—it's the algebra behind it that is the crucial factor. You'll want to use a calculator for this one.

Instructions for Birthday Algebra

Step 1: Key in your birthday month and day (for example, January 22 would be 122 or October 12 would be 1012).

Step 2: Multiply that number by 40.

Step 3: Add 1.

Step 4: Multiply the sum of Step 3 by 500.

Step 5: Add the year you were born to the results of Step 4.

Step 6: Add the year a second time.

Step 7: Subtract 500.

Step 8: Divide the results of Step 7 by 2.

The results should be the month, day, and year you were born. Here's the related algebra for this trick:

Let x = the digits of your birth month and day
Let y = the year you were born
x
$40x$
$40x + 1$
$500(40x + 1) = 20{,}000x + 500$
$20{,}000x + 500 + y$
$20{,}000x + 500 + 2y$
$20{,}000x + 2y$
$10{,}000x + y$

The end result multiplies x (the month and day) by 10,000, which moves the month and day left by four place values. When the year (y) is added, it fills the thousands, hundreds, tens, and ones places held by zeroes.

How Long Have You Lived Here? This is another interesting trick that can be explained using algebra. The algebra behind this trick is very similar to the math used in the previous trick. In both tricks, x is multiplied by a power of 10 to move it to the left. The numbers and calculations in this trick will require a calculator.

Instructions for How Long Have You Lived Here?
Step 1: Key in the house number for your address.
Step 2: Multiply the house number by 2.
Step 3: Add the number of days in a week (7) to the product of Step 2.
Step 4: Multiply that sum by 50.
Step 5: Add the number of years you've lived at this address to the results of Step 4.
Step 6: Subtract the number of days in a year (365).
Step 7: Finally add 15.

What you'll see on your calculator screen is your house number followed by 2 digits showing the number of years you've lived there. For example, if you've lived there for 5 years, it would be shown as "05."

Let's look at the algebra that makes this work:

Let x = your house number
Let y = the number of years you've lived there
x
$2x$
$2x + 7$
$50(2x + 7) = 100x + 350$
$100x + (350 + y)$
$100x + (-15 + y)$
$100x + y$

As in *Birthday Algebra*, the number represented by x is moved to the left by multiplying it by a power of 10, in this case 100. You can use similar algebra to create your own trick. For example, you could have someone

think of two numbers. The first number could be between 1 and 1,000 and the second number between 1 and 99. Try it, and you will see that it works the same way—the second number will be in the tens and ones places and the first number will be to the left.

I Know What You Rolled Here's another chance to demonstrate your amazing math magic aptitude. Your friend will roll two number cubes. Without ever seeing them, you tell what numbers were rolled on each of the two number cubes. (It's fun to do this trick blindfolded, just for effect!) After the number cubes are rolled, have your friend follow these steps.

Instructions for I Know What You Rolled

Step 1: Multiply the number on one of the cubes by 5.

Step 2: Add 7 to the product of Step 1.

Step 3: Multiply that sum by 2.

Step 4: Add the number on the other cube.

Step 5: Say the final result.

Step 6: (You do this one.) Subtract 14 from your friend's result. This will give you a two-digit number. The two digits are the numbers on the two number cubes.

This trick is really quite simple if you evaluate the algebra behind it.

Let x = one of the number cubes
Let y = the other cube
$5x$
$5x + 7$
$10x + 14$
$10x + 14 + y$
$10x + y$

As in previous tricks, a power of 10 is used to move a number to the left. In this trick, multiplying x by 10 moves the number over to the tens place, so you have one of the numbers in the tens place and the other in the ones place.

Your magical mathematical adventure is over. Try these tricks with your friends and family. I **vow** to you, your friends will be wowed. You may even find that you'll develop a real aptitude for math. When you add it all up, it's a lot of fun.

Discussion Questions

1. What are some important things to remember when performing math tricks?

2. What might happen if you got the steps of a math trick out of order? What math principle would this involve?

3. Think about the math tricks you read about. Which one was the most interesting to you? Explain.

4. Take one of the math tricks based on algebra and see if you can create a new math trick by changing some of the operations. Test your trick to make sure it will work every time.

VOCABULARY

vowed (VOWD) *v.* promised solemnly

Glossary

accelerate (ak SEL uhr ayt) *v.* speed up **25**

acquainted (uh KWAYNT ed) *adj.* familiar; known **64**

adequate (AD i kwuht) *adj.* enough for what is required or needed **29**

adjust (uh JUHST) *v.* change in order to fit or feel comfortable **26, 45**

appreciate (uh PREE shee ayt) *v.* be grateful for; understand the meaning of something **4, 50**

awed (AWD) *v.* inspired a feeling of fear and wonder **50**

background (BAK grownd) *n.* part of a movie scene that is or appears to be toward the back **51**

benefit (BEN uh fit) *n.* a gain; positive result **45, 65**

challenge (CHAL uhnj) *n.* a task requiring special effort; a dare to take part in a contest **8, 41, 60**

clarify (KLAR uh fy) *v.* make clear **36**

communicate (kuh MYOO ni kayt) *v.* make ideas or feelings known **15, 46**

compelled (KUHM peld) *v.* forced; driven **7, 48**

comprehend (kom pree HEND) *v.* grasp mentally; understand **16, 30**

context (KON tekst) *n.* the background or environment of a particular event or location **45**

deceive (dee SEEV) *v.* make someone believe something that is not true **41**

destination (des tuh NAY shuhn) *n.* place to which something is being sent or someone will arrive **7, 24**

distort (di STORT) *v.* twist an object or idea out of shape **26, 48**

emulate (EM yoo layt) *v.* equal by imitating or copying **56, 64**

epic (EP ik) *adj.* telling a story that is long and full of action; based on an epic poem, which tells the story of what gods or important people did in ancient times **48**

establish (uh STAB lish) *v.* determine; make sure of; set up **6, 44**

evidence (EV uh duhns) *n.* facts, objects, or signs that make you believe that something exists or is true **6**

evidently (ev uh DENT lee) *adv.* clearly; obviously; seemingly **7**

evoke (ee VOHK) *v.* draw a feeling, idea, or reaction out of someone **14, 48**

exceed (ek SEED) *v.* go beyond the limit or standard **16, 35**

exert (eg ZERT) *v.* put forth with force or energy **8, 36**

fantastic (fan TAS tik) *adj.* extremely good; imaginative; incredible **48**

fluent (FLOO uhnt) *adj.* able to write or speak easily and smoothly **42**

focus (FOH kuhs) *v.* fix or concentrate on one thing; adjust to make clear **56, 65**

formidable (FOHR muh duh buhl) *adj.* impressive; causing fear, dread, or awe **9**

ignorant (IG nuh ruhnt) *adj.* not knowing facts or information **24, 67**

ignored (ig NOHRD) *v.* paid no attention to **66**

impress (im PRES) *v.* put pressure on; have a lasting effect in someone's memory **9, 35, 48, 58**

improvising (IM pruh VYZ ing) *v.* making up or inventing on the spur of the moment **61**

incredible (in KRED uh buhl) *adj.* unbelievable; amazing **58**

interpret (in TER pruht) *v.* explain the meaning of something; translate **61**

intrigue (IN treeg) *n.* curiosity and interest **19, 50**

intrigue (in TREEG) *v.* arouse curiosity and interest **30**

invest (in VEST) *v.* put time, effort, or money into something for a profit or return **59**

legend (LEJ uhnd) *n.* a story handed down for generations among a people and believed to have historical basis **7**

magnificent (mag NIF uh sunt) *adj.* beautiful in a grand or stately way **13**

mature (muh CHER/TOHR) *adj.* behaving in a reasonable way; considered like an adult **59**

mystery (MIS tuh ree) *n.* something unexplained, unknown, or kept secret **11**

obvious (AHB vee uhs) *adj.* easy to see or understand; plain; evident **62**

permanent (PER muh nuhnt) *adj.* lasting for all time **7, 56**

previous (PREEV ee uhs) *adj.* occurring before in time or order **16**

prior (PRY er) *adj.* coming before in time; earlier **14**

quest (KWEST) *n.* a long search for something **14**

react (ree AKT) *v.* behave in a particular way in response to someone or something **29**

realistic (ree uh LIS tik) *adj.* showing things as they are or were in real life **53**

recall (re CAWL) *v.* call back to mind; remember **62**

recreate (ree kree AYT) *v.* make something from the past exist again in a new form or be experienced again **42**

require (ree KWYR) *v.* demand by law; deem as necessary **29, 41, 67**

resilient (ree ZIL yuhnt) *adj.* able to spring back into shape **27**

respond (ree SPAHND) *v.* reply or act in answering **35**

restrict (ree STRIKT) *v.* keep within limits **63**

resumed (ree ZOOMD) *v.* began again; continued **58**

reveal (ree VEEL) *v.* make known something hidden or kept secret **10, 32, 46, 66**

significance (sig NIF uh kuhnts) *n.* the meaning or importance of a thing, person, or idea **4**

strategy (STRAT uh jee) *n.* set of plans used to gain success or achieve an aim **58**

summoned (SUM uhnd) *v.* called together **21**

survive (ser VYV) *v.* outlive or live beyond a life-threatening event or illness **29**

transform (trans FOHRM) *v.* change **16, 26, 53, 65**

transformation (trans fohr MAY shun) *n.* a change in something or someone **15**

uncanny (uhn KAN ee) *adj.* strange; eerie **36, 54, 60**

verify (VER uh fy) *v.* prove to be true **24**

vital (VYT uhl) *adj.* extremely important; necessary **66**

vowed (VOWD) *v.* promised solemnly **74**

wonder (WUN duhr) *n.* something that makes you feel surprise and admiration **4**

Photo Credits

Cover: © Ann Lindberg/Etsa/CORBIS; **4: l.** © SCPhotos/Alamy; **4–5:** © Gary Cook/Alamy; **6–7:** © Gary Cook/Alamy; **9:** © Mary Evans Picture Library/Alamy; **10–11:** © Leonard de Selva/CORBIS; **12: l.** © Jon Arnold Images/Alamy; **12–13:** The Porcelain Tower, from an account of a Dutch Embassy to China, 1665 (engraving) by Meurs, Jacob van (c.1619–a.1680) © Private Collection/The Stapleton Collection/The Bridgeman Art Library; **14:** © Joseph Sohm; Visions of America/CORBIS; **15:** © SCPhotos/Alamy; **16–19:** © SuperStock, Inc./SuperStock; **20:** © Shigemi Numazawa/Atlas Photo Bank/Photo Researchers, Inc.; **22–25:** © Jake Socha; **26–27: t.** © Nicholas Bergkessel, Jr./Photo Researchers, Inc.; **26–27: b.** © DK Limited/CORBIS; **28:** © Jake Socha; **30–31:** © Tim MacMillan/John Downer Pr/naturepl.com; **32–34:** © Jake Socha; **36–39:** © Jake Socha; **40–41: t.** © POLYGRAM/THE KOBAL COLLECTION/BAILEY, ALEX; **40–41: b.** © TRI STAR/THE KOBAL COLLECTION; **42–43:** © Fabian Cevallos/CORBIS SYGMA; **44–45:** © CORBIS SYGMA; **46–47:** © COLUMBIA/PATHE/SONY/THE KOBAL COLLECTION; **48–49:** © John Springer Collection/CORBIS; **50–51:** © Bettmann/CORBIS; **52–53:** © Sygma/Corbis; **54–55:** © WARNER BROS./THE KOBAL COLLECTION/BAILEY, ALEX; **56–57:** © Fabian Cevallos/CORBIS SYGMA; **58: t.** © SuperStock, Inc./SuperStock; **58: b.** © Masterfile; **63:** © Map Resources 2007; **64:** © Bettmann/CORBIS; **65–66:** © Lew Robertson/JupiterImages; **69:** © Burke/Triolo Productions/Brand X/ Corbis; **70–71:** © MedioImages/Corbis; **72: l.** © Comstock/JupiterImages; **72–73:** © Dynamic Graphics/JupiterImages; **73:** © Corbis; **74: l.** © Tom Grill/ Corbis; **74–75:** © Jennifer Brown/Star Ledger/Corbis